[A DOORKNOB]

While we have sought to be accurate in presenting the
information in this book, you should always seek the
advice of a health care professional—or several profes-
sionals—for your questions and treatments. On the other
hand, you might not have confidence in them, either,
after reading this book.

Library of Congress Cataloging-in-Publication Data:
    Marston, Wendy.
        The hypochondriac's handbook /
    Wendy Marston ; photographs by Anthony
    Pardines.
        128 p. 10 x 15.2 cm.
        ISBN 0-8118-2192-7
        1. Hypochondria—Humor.
        2. Hypochondria—Popular works.
        I. Title.   RC552.H8M355 1998
    616.85'25—dc21
    98-17271   CIP

Printed in the United States of America.

Thanks to Chuck Gerba, Mitch Cohen, Lou Sorkin,
Philip Tierno, and Ann Rock.

Book design: Martine Trélaün

Distributed in Canada by Raincoast Books
9050 Shaughnessy Street
Vancouver, British Columbia V6P 6E5

    10 9 8 7 6 5 4 3

Chronicle Books LLC
85 Second Street
San Francisco, California 94105

www.chroniclebooks.com

The
Hypochondriac's
HANDBOOK

WENDY MARSTON

Photographs by Anthony Pardines

Microscopic Photographs by Andrew Syred

CHRONICLE BOOKS
SAN FRANCISCO

"At least you have your health." My relatives never missed a chance to say this, and for years, I thought nothing of it. But one day, the words took on an ominous ring: how long would I have my health? The fact that I had never been really sick, never spent a night in the hospital or broken a bone or even had a lingering cough only indicated that my good fortune couldn't last. Something was going to get me; the only questions were what and when? I became more and more cautious, more and more aware, and, eventually, totally gripped by **FEAR**.

The world is full of dangers, and disease can begin with a handshake, a vacation, a single cough, a barely noticeable twinge, an inexplicable headache. Hypochondria, I realized, is an unkind euphemism for vigilance and deserves much more respect.

Even if you seem perfectly healthy at this moment, most likely you are already sick but the symptoms may have not yet surfaced. You just need to know what to look for and what to do while you're waiting for the really serious stuff to show up. Sure that rash on your wrist could be from an aging watchband, but it could also be **PSORIASIS** or flesh-eating bacteria. How should you respond when your podiatrist offers to treat your plantar wart but says it would be painful, expensive, and unnecessary? Who can you trust to listen to your health concerns if your mother hangs up on you?

Introduction

To reassure you that you're not crazy, you're not making up your symptoms—and that you're probably not worrying enough—I've compiled this helpful handbook. Every page has enough information to keep you awake for a week, so to be sure you don't miss anything I've provided easy-to-spot "Symptom Checks" and concise but breath-taking statistics labeled "Fright Bites." Special pages are devoted to in-depth explorations of side effects for medications, **LICE**, public bathrooms, baldness, and other key troublemakers, while photographs help dramatize the everyday dangers we look at but don't really see. Across the bottom of every page is a running list of important things you should always do—or never do.

A word of warning: This book is not bathroom reading, for reasons you'll soon learn. Even if you have disinfected the entire house and sealed all doors and windows, you're still not safe. I don't want to tell you how to lead your life, but I've put in a request at the Centers for Disease Control for an Ebola bubble suit. If you aren't already wearing one, *The Hypochondriac's Handbook*, with its washable cover, might be your best defense. Carry it with you at all times. Be prepared. Don't share. **AND DON'T SAY I DIDN'T WARN YOU.**

A tapeworm can grow 20 centimeters a day in your belly. You probably won't lose any weight: they don't eat that much. More than half of the northern pike living in U.S. rivers and lakes harbor tapeworms.

FRIGHT 🐓 BITE!

30% of Americans do not wash their hands after using a public bathroom (though 9 out of 10 claim they do).

DO NOT DRINK WARM WATER FROM THE SINK: Older hot water pipes

FRIGHT 🦜 BITE!

Each year up to 33 million cases of food poisoning occur in the United States.

There are 120,000 species of fly. The common house fly, *Musca domestica*, is one of the more prevalent. It belongs to a group known as the *filth flies*, because it breeds in garbage, feces, and anything that is rotting. A female fly is able to lay 1000 or more eggs during her two-week lifetime. During a hot summer, a new generation of flies appears about every eight days. Flies carry nearly a million different strains of bacteria.

FRIGHT 🦜 BITE!

One in four office water coolers contains bacteria. The water is usually pure in the plastic container, but the faucets become contaminated.

are made of lead, which leeches into the water. **DO NOT GET A BIOPSY**

There are 120 viruses, including Hepatitis A, that live in feces. When you flush the toilet, water droplets containing more than 25,000 virus particles and 600,000 **BACTERIA FLY FROM THE BOWL**, hover for a few hours, then finally land on surfaces as far away as six feet. Closing the toilet lid won't help; the next time it's opened, a cloud of virus-carrying water particles will burst out. (Toothbrushes are a common target of this vapor.) For a truly clean toilet, regular disinfectants won't do, so you will have to spray lab alcohol in the bowl and light it. **A flambéed toilet bowl** is guaranteed to be bug free for at least one flush. *(Caution: Do not spray the alcohol on the seat and do not try this with a plastic bowl.)*

OR OTHER MEDICAL TEST ON FRIDAY: Labs are usually closed over the

[A T O I L E T]

weekend and you will have to wait till Monday for the results. ALWAYS

A Flagstaff, Arizona, teenager thought he had pulled a muscle in his groin after a long run. The next day he died of the bubonic plague. Researchers figure a flea that had bitten an infected prairie dog bit him. Plague hot spots include New Mexico, Arizona, Colorado, and California.

FRIGHT 🦜 BITE!

Women are three times more likely to have migraine headaches than men.

SIDE EFFECTS

Penicillin antibiotics (including amoxicillin, ampicillin, oxacillin, and penicillin) are prescribed to fight bacterial infections. About 10% of people are allergic to them and may develop *itching,* swelling, breathing difficulties, blood vessel collapse, skin peeling, CHILLS, fever, muscle aches, and even death.

Other possible side effects of oral penicillin are stomach upset, **VOMITING**, diarrhea, colitis, abdominal pains, coating of the tongue, and onset of fungal diseases. Side effects of injected penicillin may include dizziness, hallucinations, seizures, agitation, confusion, and anxiety.

of the shower will be on your feet, and, if dried first, will be on the

Although American scientists have assured the public that mad cow disease does not exist in domestic cows, the related Creutzfeldt-Jakob disease has appeared in deer and elk in Wyoming, Colorado, and South Dakota, affecting an estimated 5% of Colorado deer. Called chronic wasting disease, the disease may be able to jump from game to hunters who eat the meat.

FRIGHT 🐓 BITE!

There are 100,000 new cases of syphilis every year in the United States.

towel and can be wiped on the rest of your body. DO NOT BREATHE

FRIGHT  BITE!

More than 500 insect species are resistant to pesticides.

Margarine is lower in fat than butter but most brands contain trans-fatty acids, which actually raise cholesterol levels.

You wake up with more than the usual amount of "sand" in your eyes:

You forgot to take the mascara off before bed.

You sat too long in a smoky bar.

You wore contacts to bed.

You have a retinal ulcer.

Today's newspaper is usually germ-free, since fresh ink inhibits the growth of microorganisms. But yesterday's paper—or a weekly—will be covered with potentially dangerous bacteria.

WHILE USING AN AEROSOL SPRAY: Inhaling aerosol sprays or powders

[A DOG]

can cause lung damage. DO NOT HANG LAUNDRY TO DRY ON A

Almost 50% of people don't wash their hands after petting an animal, and one-third don't after coughing or sneezing. Pets carry bacteria such as *Salmonella,* insects such as ticks and fleas, and fungal infections such as ringworm, as well as roundworm and toxoplasma. All puppies carry roundworm.

FRIGHT 🐓 BITE!

Cat allergens that trigger asthma attacks were found in one out of three homes that do not have cats.

Two million Americans are bitten by dogs every year. Most victims are boys 20 and younger. About one third of those bites become infected from bacteria in the dog's mouth. Human bites can be very dangerous, too, since many of the bacteria in our mouths are resistant to antibiotics.

CLOTHESLINE IF YOU HAVE ALLERGIES: The clothes will collect pollen.

Baldness affects 40 million men and 20 million women in the United States.

The hair loss drug minoxidil must be used for life to produce results, and only works on about one-quarter of users. About three-quarters of users grow hair on the temples, between the eyebrows, on the upper cheek, and on the back, arms, and legs. Possible side effects include an itchy scalp or water and sodium retention, which can lead to heart failure.

Childbirth can spur hair loss; so can pigtails or cornrow hairstyles. Hats do not cause it.

The good news is that without hair you might not have to worry as much about the fungus *Candida*, which is carried on hair brushes and can cause yeast infections.

ALWAYS REMOVE THE FOIL ON WINE BOTTLES BEFORE REMOVING THE

FRIGHT 🎃 BITE!

The steroid Prednisone, commonly prescribed for asthma, can cause psychosis.

Urethane, produced as a byproduct of alcohol fermentation, remains in wine, fruit brandies, bourbon, scotch, sake, and other spirits. It is known to cause cancer in animals, though its effects on humans are not yet understood. Changes in alcohol production have generally meant urethane levels are dropping (since monitoring began in 1987), but older alcohols may still have high levels. How old is your scotch?

CORK: Until recently, the foil on many bottles was made with lead. DO

A reddish or furry tongue may mean scarlet fever.

A smooth, pale, glossy tongue could indicate pernicious anemia.

An extended tongue bent to the side may indicate a stroke.

Brownish sores on the tongue may indicate typhoid fever.

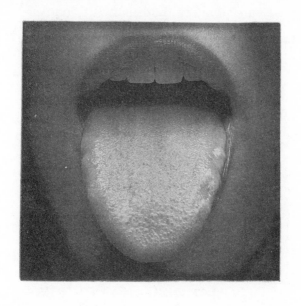

[A   T O N G U E]

tion if you arrive in an ambulance. DO NOT SHAKE HANDS WITH ANY-

"Be careful about reading health books. You may die of a misprint." —Mark Twain

FRIGHT 🐦 BITE!

Two to three drinks a day increases the risk of high blood pressure by 40%.

Mary Malone, or Typhoid Mary, a cook, was linked to 53 cases of typhoid, though she never got sick herself. There are still more than a thousand carriers of typhoid who never show symptoms. About 400 people catch the disease each year.

FRIGHT 🐦 BITE!

Snoring may reduce the passage of blood to the brain in half of all snorers, and may be a risk factor for strokes.

ONE: Hands are covered with bacteria, including Staphylococcus aureus;

FRIGHT 🐓 BITE!

We inhale between 10,000 and 20,000 liters of air a day, which contain between 10,000 and one million microorganisms.

Coccidiodes immitis is a fungus that capitalizes on dry weather. It lives in soil in warm parts of the world, and if breathed in, can cause FLU-LIKE SYMPTOMS or lie dormant for years. Vacationers have returned from visiting warm areas and two weeks later come down with this fungal infection, which in 1% of the cases leads to pneumonia. Thousands of cases occur in California; a decade ago, only a few hundred were documented. Droughts encourage the spreading of this fungus, which is carried by wind in soil particles, and regions hit by earthquakes—which stir up the fungus—also are hot spots.

viruses, including Hepatitis A; and other microorganisms (from here

Nail extenders, hardeners, and polishes can inflame the nail bed, the area where the nail meets the finger. Some hardeners and enamel contain formaldehyde, which can trigger allergic reactions. Smoking during a manicure can be hazardous: wet nail polish is flammable.

FRIGHT 🐦 BITE!

The incidence of *Salmonella* poisoning has increased 400% in the last four years.

ROUNDWORMS, or *Ascaris lumbricoides*, live in the southern United States, and can grow to more than a foot long in a human host. They flourish in human manure, or night soil, and if you breathe in roundworm eggs or eat contaminated food, the egg will mature inside the human body. If there are too many roundworms in a human host, *Ascaris lumbricoides* have been known to exit through the mouth, nose, or anus. An estimated one billion people carry roundworms.

on referred to collectively as germs). DO NOT SOAK IN A BUBBLE BATH:

FRIGHT 🦜 BITE!

There are more than 200 species of fleas in the United States. After every blood meal, female fleas lay about six eggs.

You look at the newspaper and realize the words have no meaning:

You bought *El Diario* accidentally.

You need coffee.

You are suffering from alexia, which damages the cerebral cortex, and you cannot understand written words.

Exercisers who listened to their own breathing and heartbeat felt more tired and uncomfortable than those who listened to music or just background noise.

The bubbles can irritate your skin and urinary tract. ALWAYS WASH

Two-thirds of HMOs had clauses that could be construed as restricting doctors from telling the patient everything about their cases, especially regarding drugs or services not covered by the plan. Seven percent of the plans had *non-disparaging clauses* (doctors may not undermine patient's faith in the medical plan); 32% had non-solicitation clauses (doctor can't try to persuade patient to switch plans); and 62% had confidentiality clauses (doctor prohibited from explaining the "plan's payment and incentive structure, medical management criteria, and clinical practice protocols").

FRIGHT 🗩 BITE!

A Rhode Island laboratory misread almost two dozen Pap smears in a single year. The lab recalled nearly 20,000 tests.

NEW CLOTHING BEFORE YOU WEAR IT: The material may contain abra-

FRIGHT 🦜 BITE!

Nurses and doctors wash their hands less than one-third of the time between patients.

Children bring their hands to their mouths once every three minutes, on average. The amount of dirt they swallow daily would cover seven kitchen floor tiles.

FRIGHT 🦜 BITE!

One in five Americans know their doctor's phone number by heart.

sive chemicals from manufacturing—and you don't know who else has

Notorious and final advice in Hypochondria History

"Take two aspirin and go to bed."

"You're just being hysterical. I'm going to prescribe something to calm you down."

"It's not getting any bigger."

"A good night's sleep and you'll feel better."

"It's just gas."

"That much hair always comes off on the brush."

"It's just a bruise."

"It will go away in a few days."

"You don't need stitches."

"It's just a quick little surgical procedure."

"You've never looked better."

Only 20% of people with strep throat will have classic symptoms; the rest will have no symptoms, a mild sore throat, or a condition that resembles hay fever. But nearly 3% of those with untreated strep throat get rheumatic fever, for which there is really no treatment. Rheumatic fever causes rash, lumps under the skin, tenderness in the joints, heart palpitations, and, most serious, heart failure. In 50% of the cases, patients will have deformed heart valves.

FRIGHT 🦟 BITE!

Toxic dust causes an estimated 3,000 cases of cancer a year.

The secret ingredients of most herbal "diet teas" are laxatives and a stimulant, which can lead to dehydration, arrhythmia, and even death.

OUT SOCKS: You will get blisters, be vulnerable to fungal infections,

SYMPTOM CHECK 🐝

You slept longer than usual, and have a hard time getting out of bed:

You are really tired.

You are depressed.

You have chronic fatigue syndrome.

You have lupus, an auto-immune disorder that is treatable but incurable.

You have advanced stages of chronic Chagas' disease, otherwise known as African sleeping sickness, which is spread by the tsetse fly. Some cases can be mild, but most end in coma and death.

Yelling too loudly too often can cause lesions on the vocal cords.

FRIGHT 🐦 BITE!

Sinusitis—chronic nasal congestion, frequent or constant headaches, and fatigue—increased by 50% from the late 1980s to the early 1990s.

FRIGHT 🐥 BITE!

In the United States, there are about 25 species of venomous snakes.

Washing and peeling fruit removes only one-quarter of pesticides but much of the beneficial fiber content.

COOKING: Germs on your hands spread easily to foods, especially fruits

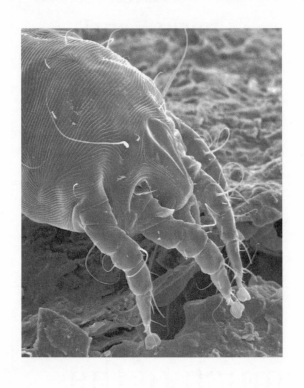

[D U S T   M I T E]

and vegetables that will be eaten uncooked. ALWAYS WASH YOUR

Living with millions of dust mites is inevitable. They make their homes in beds, floors, overstuffed couches and chairs, and stuffed animals. Clothing is also a preferred spot, serving as both vehicles for the mites to spread and movable homes. Clothing should be washed in 130 degree water, with a eucalyptus and detergent combination, which decreases the mite allergens by 95%, while dry cleaning reduces the load by only 70%. A double bed may harbor up to 2 million dust mites. A single dust mite excretes between 10 and 20 times a day. Some people are allergic to them; most are not.

HANDS AFTER COOKING: Germs from foods, especially uncooked meat

Severe halitosis could mean a lung abscess.

A few kinds of soft cheese, undercooked poultry, hot dogs incompletely reheated, and deli food have been linked to sporadic cases of listeriosis, which starts with flu-like symptoms and can develop into meningitis. Cheeses containing the *Listeriosis* bacteria include soft, white, Mexican style (such as Queso Blanco and Queso Fresco), feta, Brie, Camembert, and Roquefort.

Insect bites, scrapes, and cuts allow Group A Streptococci bacteria to get under the skin and cause impetigo, an itchy, flaky skin infection.

and chicken, spread easily to your hands. DO NOT EAT COOKIE DOUGH

James Boswell wrote 70 essays about venereal disease between 1777 and 1783. The book of essays is called *The Hypochondriack*.

FRIGHT 🐦 BITE!

Fecal bacteria was found on the hands of 20% of day-care staff workers; more than a third of day-care centers had "poor handwashing techniques."

A COLONY OF SAL-MONELLA BACTERIA CAN QUADRUPLE ITS POPULATION—IN A WARM, MOIST ENVI-RONMENT—IN LESS THAN AN HOUR.

OR BATTER IF IT CONTAINS RAW EGGS: Uncooked eggs contain new

FRIGHT 🦜 BITE!

Some bacteria can survive for months on a single dust particle.

Punto Arenas, Chile, a pleasant port city at the tip of South America, is located directly beneath the ozone hole. There are reports that rabbits go blind from UV exposure, and nearsighted salmon are easily caught.

FRIGHT 🦜 BITE!

One-third of the people who block a sneeze or cough with their hand do not then wash their hands.

strains of deadly Salmonella. DO NOT TALK ON A CELLULAR TELEPHONE

New York, New York: Bacteria found in fecal matter were identified on the screen of an automated bank machine, the back of a taxi cab, and on a headset in a 3-D movie theater. Flesh-eating bacteria were found on the mouthpiece of a pay phone. On a movie theater seat, researchers found vaginal bacteria.

FRIGHT 🦟 BITE!

The average adult will have two to three colds per year. A child will have between four and five.

Pessimists not only see their lot as tougher than optimists, but are actually sicker. A recent study showed that pessimists at age 25 had poorer health at age 45.

WHILE DRIVING A CAR: Your chance of having an accident increases

Your feet reek and your toenails are yellowing:

You need new shoes.

You have a case of athlete's foot and toenail fungus.

It's the early stage of gangrene.

Residents of Manila have a 15% higher risk of lung cancer than people in other cities. Seventy-three percent of Manila's citizens smoke.

FRIGHT 🦜 BITE!

65% of American adolescents will get acne. Not getting it then doesn't mean you won't get it as an adult.

Fava bean allergies can cause Favism (not to be confused with Fauvism, which occurs in artists), that can provoke acute hemolysis, the dissolution of red blood cells.

Are you always the most interesting person in the room? Is everyone else boring, except when they talk about you? Are you brilliant, beautiful, or both? You might have narcissistic personality disorder.

Women's Restrooms

Public women's restrooms are twice as germ-laden as men's. Women spend more time in the bathroom, and also bring in children, a.k.a., walking, talking bacterial hot zones.

The dirtiest places are, in order: exterior of the sanitary napkin disposal bin; floor around the toilet; the sink and taps; toilet seat; flush handle.

48% of women line the toilet seat with either the paper seat covers or with toilet paper.

American women use the most toilet paper in the world—seven sheets per visit—while the British come in second—3.9 sheets per visit.

The middle stall in a public bathroom is usually the most contaminated, while the first is the least contaminated.

The fungus *Aspergillus fumigatus* is found nearly everywhere, including bread mold and in soil, and preys on people susceptible to allergies. But it is especially dangerous to those with compromised immune systems, so hospital patients recovering from organ transplants and chemotherapy are at risk: 4% of kidney transplant patients and 6% of bone-marrow transplant patients get aspergillus infections. Because the fungus moves through the body from tissue to tissue and avoids the bloodstream, diagnosis is difficult and many patients die before doctors know what went wrong.

FRIGHT 🦇 BITE!

Male cats provoke more and stronger allergic reactions in humans than females.

YOUR ELBOW: Sharp objects can puncture an eardrum, and cotton

FRIGHT 🐦 BITE!

17% of homes in the United States have unsafe levels of radon.

Penis **ENLARGEMENTS** take only about half an hour to perform. The most common method is to remove fat from another part of the body and inject it into the penis. The surgeon also releases the ligaments at the base of the penis, which allows it to lengthen. But in many cases, problems develop, including impotence and scarring. And sometimes the fat injections don't stay put.

FRIGHT 🐦 BITE!

A baby in an American city will ingest, on average—from dust and residues of cleaning products—toxic chemicals equivalent to smoking three cigarettes a day.

---

swabs just push the wax in deeper. DO NOT PUT ON A SHIRT OR JACKET

FRIGHT 🐔 BITE!

Obstetricians-gynecologists have one of the highest rates of being sued for malpractice.

By age 30, 4 out of 10 Americans will have cold sores on their lips, which are caused by herpes simplex virus type-one, or HSV-1. These sores can be triggered by a cold, too much sun, or stress. They are contagious and there is no cure. Half of the population will have canker sores—ulcers in the mouth's mucous membranes—during their lifetime. Researchers do not know what causes them.

Makeup

If you test makeup products in a store, first wipe off the surface of the product, then use a Q-Tip for the sample. The preservatives in makeup kill off bacteria over the course of a day, but preservatives in cosmetics used by the public won't be able to keep up.

Putting on mascara while in a mov-ing vehicle can be very dangerous. If you slip and the wand goes into your eye, severe infection can result, since an eyeball scratch allows airborne bacteria and other substances to enter.

"Hypoallergenic" is not a technical term, but means only that the manufacturer thinks the product is not likely to provoke an allergic reaction.

"Natural," when referring to cos-metics, can mean almost anything. A plant used in the production of cosmetics can be tainted with bacteria, pesticides, and other substances.

If you get conjunctivitis, throw away all your eye makeup.

[M A K E U P]

OR BATH: The bacteria in your own bathroom are yours and won't hurt

FRIGHT 🐓 BITE!

Houseflies, which visit both food and feces, are prime transmitters of bacteria.

If you are allergic to cows or milk, think twice about that collagen injection you want to make your lips more pouty. Collagen is often derived from cattle.

In many American homes, the toilet may be cleaner than the kitchen sink. The reason is that people use disinfectants on toilets but allow sponges and food residue to remain in kitchen sinks for days, even weeks. Fecal bacteria are often, if not always, found in kitchen sinks.

you, but introducing microbial fauna from others can give you infec-

Vitiligo affects 1 to 2% of the population, causing white patches to appear and spread on the skin. **MICHAEL JACKSON** claims to have this ailment.

FRIGHT 🦜 BITE!

In the fall of 1997, thousands of fish with open sores died in the Pocomoke River in Maryland. Fishermen and waterskiers suffered memory loss, rashes, and shortness of breath.

Women injure their knees eight times as often as men, and in the last five years, athletic women injured their anterior cruciate ligaments (ACL) six times as frequently as men.

tions. DO NOT RELY ON WEARING SANDALS TO PREVENT THE SPREAD

Cockroaches

The world is home to over 3,500 species of cockroaches. They shed their exoskeleton several times a year. In some species, a female will mate once and remain pregnant for the rest of her life. If it doesn't bleed to death, a roach can live for weeks without a head. Roaches can swim and run up to three miles per hour. Juvenile roaches can squeeze through a dime-thin crack, while adults need the space of the width of a quarter. Roaches can climb straight up a wall. They have recently been linked to skyrocketing rates of asthma and allergies: their droppings and secretions are powerful allergens.

German cockroaches can produce 3,200 babies in five months.

A cockroach breaks wind every quarter of an hour.

FRIGHT 🦇 BITE!

One out of 10 Americans generally, and 4 out of 10 people who have allergies, are allergic to dogs or cats. Cat allergies are twice as common as dog allergies. More than 50% of American homes have a cat or dog.

Nausea, dizziness, headaches, and diarrhea may be due to methyl parathion, a nerve gas used by exterminators increasingly—and illegally—in this country to kill bugs. Pets, who live closer to the ground, are usually the first to get sick.

After a long night of drinking, you swear that petite beings with elongated limbs and wide staring eyes abducted you:

Your friends creatively shaped your drunken experience.

You were abducted, a relatively pleasant experience that nearly four million Americans claim happened to them.

You are suffering from a symptom of Korsakoff's psychosis, which follows postalcoholic tremors, and really believe that last night's episode of the X Files happened to you.

SYMPTOM CHECK 💊

and using antifungal powders are more effective. DO NOT USE HAIR

One way of removing annoying insects from the ear canal, according to a medical manual, is to fill the canal with mineral oil. This kills the insect, providing prompt relief and easy removal of its body with forceps.

FRIGHT 🐦 BITE!

Catheters are prime sites for infection.

Worldwide, 400 million people a year contract malaria, which is spread by mosquitoes; between one and three million people die from it annually. Ninety percent of malaria cases occur in Africa, but travelers can start small outbreaks anywhere mosquitoes live. Malaria is becoming resistant to vaccines.

FRIGHT 🐦 BITE!

Cases of sudden deafness with no apparent cause strike about one out of 5,000 people every year.

SPRAY AFTER PUTTING IN CONTACT LENSES: The spray can coat the

FRIGHT 🦇 BITE!

Infanticide by a stepparent is sixty times as high as those by a biological parent, while sexual abuse is eight times as high.

It may be cheaper to install a hot-air hand dryer in a public restroom than to provide towels, but it isn't necessarily cleaner. Blowing dryers gather bacteria from the air and propel them onto your hands.

lenses and cause irritation and infection. DO NOT ALLOW YOUR TOOTH-

Procrastinators had 20% more headaches, colds, and stomachaches than those who got things done on time; they also visited doctors 60% more often. Procrastinating students had grades a whole letter higher than timely students, however.

FRIGHT 🐦 BITE!

Visitors to and residents of Las Vegas are two-and-a-half times likelier to kill themselves than people in other, non-gambling cities; Atlantic City visitors and residents are one-and-a-third times more likely to commit suicide.

Kissing a sick person is safer than shaking their hand. Most germs are distributed via hands, then from hands to mouths, noses, and eyes.

BRUSH TO TOUCH ANOTHER TOOTHBRUSH: Germs spread. ALWAYS

You've been taking antibiotics for a cold but since you are feeling much better you have a burger. In that (medium-rare) burger are a few antibiotic resistant *Salmonella* bacteria. Once in your stomach and small intestine, the *Salmonella* find the competition nil, since it's been destroyed by the antibiotics. They quickly reproduce, and you are out for the next few days vomiting.

WEAR A BANDAGE ON A CUT, NO MATTER HOW SMALL: Tetanus germs,

Side Effects

Diazepam is the generic name of a drug prescribed for the relief of anxiety, tension, or fatigue and sold under a variety of brand names, including Valium and Zetran. Possible side effects are: confusion, depression, lethargy, headache, disorientation, dizziness, constipation, nausea, dry mouth, incontinence, irregular heart rhythm, change in sex drive, lowered blood pressure, blurred vision, rash, fluid retention, nervousness, hiccups, and insomnia.

as well as others, can enter the body through a wound. DO NOT USE

FRIGHT 🐦 BITE!

Lyme disease, which initially causes a red, bull's eye–shaped rash in some people and progresses to an arthritic-like condition, has increased 20-fold since 1980. Dogs are also susceptible to Lyme disease.

Hepatitis B has been transmitted via office filing cabinets; workers got the disease through paper cuts. Sharing towels and toothbrushes are easier ways to contract the disease.

Half of those who got chicken pox as kids and who live to 85 will get shingles, caused by the latent chicken pox virus. Shingles sufferers can spread chicken pox to those who haven't had it yet.

THE SAME CUTTING BOARD FOR UNCOOKED MEAT AND CHICKEN THAT

[F I S H]

YOU USE FOR OTHER FOODS: Bacteria, including Salmonella, from raw

ALTHOUGH THE USE OF PCBs WAS DIS-CONTINUED IN 1972, THOSE TOXIC CHEMI-CALS ARE STILL FOUND IN FISH.

FRIGHT 🦎 BITE!

Every day 2,700 Americans are told they have gonorrhea.

Except for one family, all spiders are venomous. Only about 60 species have jaws and fangs that can **PENETRATE** human skin.

USE A FRESHLY LAUNDERED DISH TOWEL EVERY DAY: Bacteria begin

Teenagers who have trouble getting out of bed might not be lazy. Kleine-Levin syndrome, a rare disorder that strikes teenage boys, can cause sufferers to sleep for as long as 17 days. There is no cure.

FRIGHT 🦜 BITE!

From 1982 to 1992, the incidence of asthma rose by 42%.

Testosterone, the male sex hormone, drops 1 to 2% a year in men who are 30 and older. Half of all men between the ages of 75 and 80 have abnormally low testosterone. But, testosterone supplements may not be a good idea: the hormone is known to increase growth of prostate cancer and excess testosterone may increase stroke risk. Men who took testosterone supplements also reported mood swings. The hormone will boost libido but doesn't help performance.

to grow on the towel the first time you use it, especially after you dry

FRIGHT 🦜 BITE!

4% of Americans have giardiasis, a parasite in water and food that causes diarrhea, flatulence, and other problems.

A study done in the early 1990s showed that the number of fecal bacteria in a hotel bathroom doubled when the room cost less than $40 per night. (Today, after inflation, that dollar amount would be slightly higher.)

FRIGHT 🦜 BITE!

70% of people with colds have infectious material on their hands.

your hands, and they multiply significantly overnight. WHEN ENTERING

Jews and Italians are more likely to complain about pain than Anglo-Saxons and Irish Catholics.

A PUBLIC BATHROOM, DO NOT TOUCH THE DOOR HANDLE, THE LATCH

Berry aneurysms, which form at the base of the brain, can burst at any time and result in hemorrhagic strokes that strike 30,000 Americans each year. One out of three attacks occurs during sleep, and half of those result in instant death, most commonly in people 40 to 60 years old. Warning signs include headaches, nausea, and stiff neck, but in nine out of ten cases, there will be no warning symptoms.

FRIGHT 🐔 BITE!

Every year, about 2,000 Japanese people get sick from worms in raw fish. The United States does not keep those statistics.

Flu viruses can live for years in dried spit.

ON THE STALL DOOR, THE TOILET SEAT, THE FLUSHER HANDLE, THE

You have hiccups that won't go away:

You swallowed some air.   You have bowel disease.

You are pregnant.   You have pneumonia.

You are an alcoholic.

International travelers are often warned to avoid the water as well as fresh vegetables when visiting developing countries. More than a quarter of vegetables and fruits sold in the United States are imported from developing countries. Many parasites found in this produce are increasingly resistant to pesticides.

FAUCET, THE SOAP DISPENSER, THE HOT-AIR BLOWER, OR THE DOOR

In the United States, 50 million people suffer from autoimmune disorders, such as multiple sclerosis, arthritis, lupus, and more than fifty others. Doctors do not know why these diseases, in which the body's immune system turns on itself occur, but on average, someone with these problems will see an average of six doctors over a period of five years before getting a correct diagnosis.

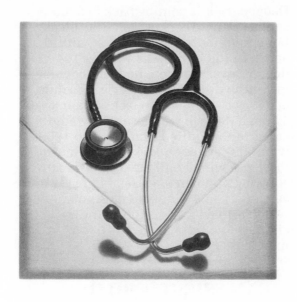

[M E D I C A L I N S T R U M E N T S]

PROTECTION: Even high sun-protection factor (SPF) blocks do not

Dengue fever is coming back in a more serious form. Also known as the breakbone fever because it causes painful aches in the joints—as well as 104 degree fever, nausea, headache, and rash—the disease spreads via mosquito and is very common in tropical climates. Though dengue was essentially eradicated in the United States in the 1960s, when its carrier (*Aedes aegypti* mosquitoes) was wiped out, the disease is now showing up in an often fatal form. The carrier is the Asian tiger mosquito, which arrived in Houston in the mid-eighties and now makes its home in at least 17 states.

FRIGHT 🐦 BITE!

A quarter of midwestern homes in the United States have DDT in their carpets. DDT was banned in 1972.

Ear infections are encouraged by getting water or other irritants, such as hair spray or dye, in the ear. Cotton swabs do not clean the ear but instead push earwax deeper inside, promoting infection and disrupting the ear's natural cleaning cycle.

shield you from dangerous ultraviolet rays that can cause skin cancers.

There is no such thing as a 24-hour *stomach virus.* Most likely, it is a case of food-borne illness—**FOOD POISONING**—caused by bacteria.

DO NOT EAT COOKED CHICKEN OR TURKEY KEPT ON THE BONE FOR

FRIGHT 🦜 BITE!

Half of the world's population is infected with tuberculosis.

Histoplasmasis capsulatum is a fungus found along all major waterways in North America. It breeds in bird and bat droppings, which dry, are blown around by wind, and are inhaled. The fungus can be dormant for years before a person becomes ill, allowing the fungus to migrate through the body, causing systemic infection (often, flu-like symptoms). About 200,000 new cases per year develop in the United States; archaeologists and spelunkers (cave explorers) are at higher risk than others.

FRIGHT 🦜 BITE!

Having even a mild ear infection while flying on an airplane can result in tympanic membrane ruptures, or imploded eardrums.

MORE THAN THREE DAYS, AND DO NOT EAT AT ALL AFTER FIVE DAYS:

Charles Darwin suffered from severe anxiety, headaches, intestinal problems, and fatigue, but was somewhat pleased with the results of his perceived ill-health/hypochondria. *"Even ill-health, though it has annihilated several years of my life, has saved me from the distractions of society and amusement."*

In her mid 30s, Florence Night-ingale returned from the Crimean War and announced she was going to die. She made a will, got in bed, then got interested in new projects and lived into her 90s. *"Her illness, whatever it may have been, was not inconvenient,"* wrote Lytton Strachey in *Eminent Victorians.*

From *Phantom Illness*, by Carla Cantor with Brian Fallon: *"Why is hypochondria something we turn away from?"*

Smoking 2 cigars a day is equivalent to smoking a pack of cigarettes a day. Cigar smokers have 4 to 10 times the chances of non-smokers of dying from cancer of the mouth, larynx, or esophagus. An eight-inch-long cigar has forty times the nicotine in a cigarette. A quarter of U.S. teenagers between the ages of 14 and 19 smoked at least 1 cigar last year, and 3.9% of the boys and 1.2% of the girls smoked 50 cigars during the previous year.

FRIGHT 🐦 BITE!

Fresh goat cheese is the most common source of *Brucella*, a bacteria which causes fever, chills, and depression.

DO NOT SCRATCH A SCAB: You may open the wound to new infection.

Schistosomiasis is a disease caused by blood flukes that live in fresh water, mostly in the tropics. The cercariae penetrate the skin while a person is bathing or swimming, then go through the heart and lungs, settle in the liver to mature, and mate in the intestines. After a few days a rash appears, and within a month fever, chills, cough, and muscle aches may set in, though most people **EXHIBIT NO SYMPTOMS** after the initial rash in the early phase after infection. If the infection is not diagnosed, the parasite can damage the liver, intestines, lungs, or bladder. About 200 million people worldwide are infected, causing 200,000 deaths a year.

FRIGHT 🐓 BITE!

Baby turtles, which are illegal to buy in the United States, were responsible for 14% of the salmonellosis cases in a single year.

DO NOT EAT A BIG MEAL RIGHT BEFORE GOING TO SLEEP: It is harder to

---

*Too much of
a good thing*

Products used every day can cause contact dermatitis, or a rash instigated by a substance you are not allergic to but that actually damages the skin. Common culprits are:

1. Nail polish, which causes eyelid dermatitis if a person touches her eyes with her fingers before two hours have elapsed (the time it takes for the polish to dry).

2. Lipstick, toothpaste, and chapped lip ointments.

3. Deodorants.

4. Antistatic laundry products.

5. Nickel, a ubiquitous metal in jewelry that is also used in bra fasteners.

6. Eyelash curlers.

7. Eyeglass frames.

8. Acne medications.

Your hair is really dry and flyaway, and there seems to be a lot more of it in your brush:

You should change shampoos.

You take after your mother's father, hairline and all. Rogaine may help—or not.

You may be overdosing on vitamin A.

You may be in the early stages of syphilis.

FRIGHT 🐛 BITE!

Between 1985 and 1992, the number of prescriptions for middle ear infections increased by 50%, from 15 million to 23 million.

The warning for Hydrocodone-Ibuprofen (ibuprofen and synthetic codeine) commonly used for pain includes the following side effects: mild headache, dizziness, drowsiness, nausea, or constipation. Less likely side effects: stomach pain, irregular or shallow breathing, or unusual bleeding or bruising. Very unlikely side effects: black stools or "coffee ground" vomiting, yellowing eyes or skin, unusual change in the quantity of urine, accelerated heartbeat, fever, severe headache, stiff neck, ringing in the ears, mood changes.

OFF THE TOP OF A CAN OF SODA BEFORE DRINKING, ESPECIALLY IF

The differences between the male and female genders are not always cut and dried. In between are HERMS (for hermaphrodites, who have both male and female genitals and produce both sperm and eggs), MERMS (who have both male and female genitals but cannot produce eggs), and FERMS, (who can produce eggs but no sperm, and have both male and female genitals). Many hermaphrodites are surgically altered at birth and never know their condition.

FRIGHT 🦜 BITE!

Divorced, single, widowed, or separated people are more likely to have symptoms or diseases than married people.

YOU DRINK FROM THE CAN: Soda cans have a long and varied history

FRIGHT 🐓 BITE!

The number of people without medical insurance now exceeds 40 million; of these, 10 million are children.

The worm *Anisakis simplex*, which measures only half an inch long and prefers to live in seal stomachs, can make its way into human hosts via sushi. The symptoms it prompts are often misdiagnosed as stomach cancer or appendicitis.

People who do not drink, do not smoke, do not engage in sex, do not consume more than 25 grams of saturated fat per day, and who exercise aerobically at least five times a week do not necessarily live longer: it only seems longer.

before they make their way to your lips, and they carry a particularly

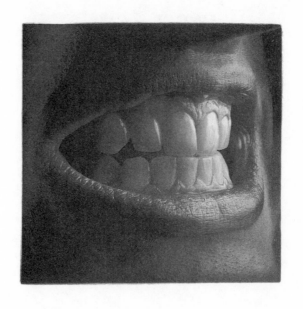

[G U M S]

wide assortment of germs. DO NOT USE A KITCHEN SPONGE TO WIPE

Thus far, there's been only a single documented case of someone getting AIDS from kissing. But three-quarters of Americans older than 35 have gum disease, causing many of them to bleed from the gums and thus be more likely to pass infections—including HIV—through kissing.

PLATES OR SILVERWARE: Sponges are the petri-dishes-with-holes of the

FRIGHT 🐓 BITE!

In one year, more than 6,000 men had breast reduction surgery.

Are you too fat? Too thin? Did you buy your floor-length mirror for $9.99 and then congratulate yourself on your savvy consumer skills? Unfortunately, studies show that unless you spent about $7 dollars per square foot on that looking glass, you aren't getting an accurate vision of yourself.

FRIGHT 🐓 BITE!

Sitting puts 40% more pressure on the disks of your lower spine than standing.

household, serving as excellent breeding grounds for bacteria. ALWAYS

FRIGHT 🐓 BITE!

Losing 100 strands of hair a day is normal.

Your desk is gleaming, papers piled neatly, everything done on time. Your sock drawer is arranged by color and by fluffiness. Your dog matches the interior of your car. The bad news? You may be a bit too well-organized and may have a touch of obsessive-compulsive disorder.

LAUGH, EAT SPICY FOOD, AND EXERCISE AEROBICALLY: Each activity

Rosacea is a skin disorder affecting 5% of Americans, though it often goes undiagnosed. It is more common in fair-skinned people between the ages of 30 and 50, and hits more women than men. People who have always had **CLEAR SKIN** may be more susceptible to rosacea; so are those of Irish, English, or Eastern European descent. Using corticosteroids can trigger the disorder. Symptoms resemble severe acne. If left untreated, rosacea may develop into rhinophyma, which can lead to a bulbous, red nose (W.C. Fields had this problem). Rosacea can also cause burning, gritty eyes and affect vision. People with rosacea are more likely to have problems with the ubiquitous *Demodex folliculorum*, microscopic mites that eat dead, flaking skin cells.

SYMPTOM CHECK

Having a dry mouth can be a symptom of:

Anemia.	Infected salivary glands.
Diabetes.	Stress.

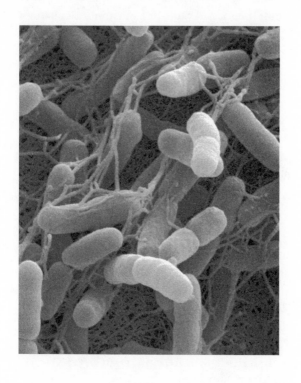

[BACTERIA ON A DISHCLOTH]

AN AIRPLANE: Alcohol, like caffeine, increases the chances of a pul-

Smelling a bad odor others cannot detect is a condition called dysosmia, and may indicate:

Infected nasal passages.

Depression.

A zinc deficiency.
(Dysgueusia, or a distorted sense of taste, may also be caused by a zinc deficiency.)

Although the United States stopped inventing biological weapons in 1969, the Soviets did not. Outside of one biological-weapons factory in Russia, scientists found mice carrying a strain of lab-developed bacteria that causes pneumonia. A pipe was leaking the bacteria into the ground. Researchers assume the bacteria are still among the rodents in that region, and perhaps beyond. The disease may spread from rodents to humans.

FRIGHT 🐦 BITE!

Smoking doubles the risk of bladder cancer.

FRIGHT 🦜 BITE!

Hypochondria is most common among people in their 20s and 30s.

Ask for a window seat on an airplane: injuries from falling objects from overhead bins can cause serious accidents, 9 out of 10 of them to the head. More than a third of these require medical attention.

FRIGHT 🦜 BITE!

Toxic algae blooms in seas and oceans are increasing all over the world. The **"red tide"** can be harmful if eaten directly, or even if ingested through the food chain.

ONDS BEFORE DRINKING: Bacteria and other germs that accumulate in

Rodents make up more than a quarter of all mammal species and can live in nearly any habitat. Rats breed quickly—one female can give birth to more than 100 babies a year. Some species, specifically the Norway rat, are found almost anywhere people live. The Black Death, or bubonic plague, has killed hundreds of millions of people. Today, about 7,000 people worldwide die of plague every year. The bacteria that causes plague is transmitted to humans from rats via a flea bite, then from person to person through inhaling an infected person's breath. Rats also transmit rat-bite fever (passed along in about 10% of all rat bites), typhus, murine typhus, and scores of other infectious diseases.

the pipes and faucet need to be flushed out. DO NOT USE SOMEONE

FRIGHT 🐤 BITE!

FBI healthcare fraud investigations increased five-fold from 1991 to 1996.

If your salon isn't clean, you have about a 2% chance of getting a herpes infection or a pimple-causing staph infection while getting a facial. Make sure the facialist is wearing new latex gloves. And if you have a cut, you are twice as likely to get an infection during a manicure or pedicure.

FRIGHT 🐤 BITE!

A fine black line on the gums is a serious indication of chronic lead poisoning.

Are you living up to your potential? Are you haunted by a sneaking suspicion that you could be doing much better? Did your mom smoke when she was pregnant with you? If yes, then don't be so hard on yourself. Babies born to smoking moms have smaller heads and don't develop math and verbal skills as well as their cohorts whose moms abstained. As for dads, babies fathered by smoking dads have more than a 40% higher rate of getting childhood cancers.

AN AIRPLANE OR IN A THEATER OR A MUSIC STORE: Germs. DO

FRIGHT 🐦 BITE!

Facial expressions affect mood. Frowning can contribute to feelings of unhappiness.

Between 10 and 12 million new cases of sexually transmitted diseases are reported annually in the United States. Someone with herpes, syphilis, gonorrhea, and chlamydia is more than twice as likely to contract HIV than an uninfected person. One out of ten Americans over the age of 12 is infected with genital herpes.

FRIGHT 🐦 BITE!

More than half of the raw chickens in U.S. supermarkets have *Campylobacter*, which causes 5 to 14% of diarrhea cases. *Campylobacter* may be linked to Guillain-Barré syndrome, a rare and potentially fatal nerve disorder.

NOT TOUCH THE METAL OF A TURNSTILE: Germs. DO NOT LIE NAKED

Drugs to treat victims of heart attacks should be given within 30 minutes of the patient's arrival in the ER, but on average the wait was 50 minutes for men and 56 minutes for women.

FRIGHT 🦟 BITE!

One-third of THC from marijuana remains in the body after smoking, and can affect the body's functions three weeks later.

FRIGHT 🐦 BITE!

Showering bombards us with hundreds of thousands of droplets of water; each droplet contains hundreds of thousands of bacteria.

Most people who are depressed also manifest hypochondriacal symptoms.

FRIGHT 🐦 BITE!

One half of all outpatient antibiotic prescriptions are inappropriate.

OTHER PEOPLE'S BOWLING SHOES: Germs. DO NOT LEAN YOUR

The bacteria that causes Hansen's disease, or leprosy, lives only in humans and armadillos. About 15% of all American armadillos are suspected of carrying the bacteria.

From a letter by Marcel Proust:

"DEAR FRIEND, I HAVE NEARLY DIED THREE TIMES SINCE MORNING."

HEAD BACK AGAINST THE SEAT IN A MOVIE THEATER: Germs.

Thousands of Milwaukee residents came down with diarrhea after drinking water infested with the parasite *Cryptosporidium*, found in cow feces. High spring runoff rushing into Lake Michigan from dairy farms and slaughterhouses was the culprit.

FRIGHT 🐦 BITE!

Only in four states can a private U.S. citizen find out if his or her physician has settled a malpractice case.

Running or walking on a grass or dirt trail is most likely to cause injury. Beaches are the next most likely to hurt you, while flat cinder tracks are the safest.

FRIGHT 🐦 BITE!

Spongy gums can be a sign of chronic mercury poisoning.

DO NOT DRINK FROM A WATER FOUNTAIN AND CERTAINLY DO

Unbroken eggs are becoming a major source of *Salmonella* bacteria. In the 1960s, researchers thought the bacteria lived in chicken feces and penetrated the shell, but now they find *Salmonella* bacteria—a newly evolved strain—within the yolk. Most Americans eat egg products daily.

NOT LET YOUR LIPS TOUCH ANY PART OF THE FOUNTAIN: Germs. DO

[A N E G G]

NOT LET A DOG LICK YOU ON THE FACE: Germs. DO NOT USE SOME-

Rabies

The rabies virus is carried by most carnivores—raccoons, dogs, coyotes, foxes, skunks—as well as bats, and as animal populations grow and humans encroach on their property, the risk increases. There are 7,000 to 10,000 human rabies cases per year and 10,000 documented animal cases, which is probably around one-tenth of the real number. Raccoons are the prime carriers now. Although rabies can be treated, the shot must be given soon after the bite and before symptoms appear. If a bite goes untreated and symptoms appear (between 10 days and a year, a victim becomes depressed, restless, feverish, then uncontrollably excited, with drooling and twitching), there is no cure. Rabies, at that point, is fatal.

WOBBLY HANDWRITING is one of the earliest symptoms of Wilson's disease, a genetic disorder in which the patient has many times the normal amount of copper in his body. Early symptoms include tremors in the extremities—which causes bad handwriting—and become apparent between ages five and fifty. Wilson's disease is fatal unless diagnosed and treated.

FRIGHT 🐦 BITE!

The head of a major medical manufacturer was recently sentenced to more than a year in jail after selling thousands of unsterilized gynecological instruments.

Eight out of 10 Americans will have lower back pain during their lifetimes. Half of the workforce will suffer from it in any given year. One insurance company determined that 33% of its total claim expenses went to cover lower back pain.

DO NOT USE A PUBLIC TELEPHONE: Germs are aimed at your ear as

More than 80 food-borne parasites exist. Not only are the parasites themselves a problem, their secretions and excretions can also make us sick. Even after worms are removed from food, such as vegetables, their waste products may remain, causing health problems.

FRIGHT 🦜 BITE!

Women are twice as likely as men to have panic attacks.

Ergot poisoning is not a disease of philosophers. It comes from eating grain contaminated by *Claviceps purpurea*, the ergot fungus, which can cause hallucinations.

well as your mouth. ALWAYS WASH YOUR HANDS BEFORE WASHING

Each year 8,000 Americans are bitten by venomous snakes, and 9 to 15 die. The antivenin used to counteract the bite is made from a serum derived from horse blood. Most people treated with antivenin will develop a sensitivity to horses and horse products, including estrogen, used in hormone replacement therapies.

FRIGHT 🐔 BITE!

Brainerd diarrhea has no known cause and researchers still don't know how it is spread. Sufferers experience explosive diarrhea 3 to 20 times a day for more than a month. There is no cure. Seven outbreaks of Brainerd diarrhea have occurred since 1983.

A fifth of the world's population carries hookworms, and most carriers have no symptoms. Hookworms enter the human body through the feet, travel through the bloodstream to the lungs, then into the intestines. Hookworm causes symptoms similar to ulcers.

There is no known cause of or cure for interstitial cystitis, or frequent urination, a syndrome that causes some to urinate between 20 and 40 times a day. IC affects about 450,000 Americans. The average age of onset is 40, and nine out of 10 sufferers are men. Thirty percent of those with IC cannot work outside of the home.

FRIGHT 🦟 BITE!

About 1 million women per year develop pelvic inflammatory disease, many after having undiagnosed chlamydia or gonorrhea. 10% will be infertile as a result.

Yersinia, which causes diarrhea, is found in water, milk, vegetables, seafood, and poultry. It can reproduce even in refrigerators and cause symptoms similar to appendicitis.

FRIGHT 🦟 BITE!

First-born women are more likely to be hypochondriacs than women who have older siblings.

tepid water and mild soaps to avoid drying your skin. DO NOT WRITE

[K I T C H E N   S I N K]

WITH INK ON YOUR BODY: You won't die of ink poisoning unless you

More than

90% of kitchen

sinks harbor

Salmonella

and Campy-

lobacter.

are writing a novel, but the ink as well as the soap and the rubbing

To disinfect your kitchen sink, fill it with water and bleach, or water and disinfectant, and soak sponges for twenty minutes. Washing and rinsing a cutting board will not kill germs. To banish bacteria left from meat or unwashed vegetables, use bleach and hot water. Soak cutting boards weekly.

SYMPTOM CHECK

Seeing "sparks" followed by floaters in the eye may mean your retina has become detached.

you'll do to remove the ink are abrasive to the skin. ALWAYS WEAR A

FRIGHT 🐦 BITE!

Adults will have one and a half cases of diarrhea per year. A child will have three.

Three percent (more than 7 million) of Americans own pet reptiles. Reptiles carry *Salmonella* in their intestinal tracts, which can infect people. Twenty people came down with salminellosis, which can lead to blood infections, meningitis, and death, after visiting a zoo where Komodo dragons were on display. The dragons had apparently licked some of their cages, which the visitors touched, who then ate lunch without washing their hands.

FRIGHT 🐦 BITE!

After a tragedy or an accident, 25% of people will suffer from post-traumatic stress syndrome, which can include insomnia, depression, and anxiety.

COTTON MASK WHILE PUMPING GAS: Gas fumes increase carcinogen lev-

FRIGHT 🦔 BITE!

In 1966, fewer than 25,000 Americans visited their doctors because they had contracted genital herpes. Now, nearly 500,000 cases are diagnosed annually. More than 30 million Americans are infected.

Raynaud's phenomenon affects almost 10% of Americans, making blood vessels in fingers, toes, earlobes, lips, and the nose constrict, turning skin red, white, and blue, as well as causing numbing and throbbing. Serious effects, besides discomfort, are sores and gangrene.

FRIGHT 🦔 BITE!

More than a million children under the age of five are eating fruit, including baby food, that contains unsafe levels of pesticides.

els in the blood. DO NOT SWIM IN A POOL THAT DOES NOT HAVE CHLORINE:

Tooth brushing grinds thousands of microorganisms into your gums and thus into your circulatory systems.

You have always been so healthy! You've had all your shots and all your boosters. You exercise, drink exactly one (if you are female) or two (if you are male) glasses of red wine a day. You eat vegetables and fruit. You are easygoing. You like your job. You give money to public radio. You floss. And you have a very good chance of getting asthma. People who had more infections as a child—thus flexing their immune systems—are half as likely to develop asthma.

Chlorine disinfects the water and kills most (though not all) germs. **DO NOT**

You know you're
a Hypochondriac
when

You carry a sphygmomanometer in your back pack.

You stay in your doctor's waiting room after your exam to explain your symptoms to other patients.

You've exhausted all the drugstores in town that give free cholesterol tests.

You wash your hands up to the elbows at least ten times a day.

You take at least three of the fol-lowing daily: ginko; 1,500 grams of vitamin C; three garlic pills; two St. John's Wort; shark's cartilage; bilberry pills; spirulina; criotine; vitamin E; Serbian ginseng; and 500 mg. of echinacea.

You're afraid of catching a com-puter virus.

You buy latex gloves in bulk.

SWIM IN A POOL THAT HAS CHLORINE: Chlorine is harmful to the eyes and

FRIGHT 🦜 BITE!

Coliform bacteria was found on 60% of office coffee mugs. Ten percent had *E. coli.*

Pollen allergies affect more than 30 million people. A pollen particle is tiny, smaller than the width of a human hair, and is easily carried by the breeze. On heavy pollen days, sufferers shouldn't do strenuous activity outside between 5 a.m. and 10 p.m. and should stay indoors on windy days. Before leaving the house, check the web site http://www. aaaai.org/docs/nab/pollen.htm or call 1-800-9-POLLEN to see what the pollen counts are for your region.

FRIGHT 🦜 BITE!

300,000 injuries—including 80,000 deaths—each year occur in hospitals due to negligence.

skin and may be poisonous if swallowed. ALWAYS WEAR MOSQUITO REPEL-

A single pair of underwear contains an average of one-tenth to 10 grams of fecal matter consisting of, among other things, the rotavirus, which causes diarrhea, and the hepatitis virus. *Washing underwear with other clothes* simply distributes the fecal matter through the load. Infection from this matter most likely occurs while the clothes are being moved from the washer to the dryer; the dryer usually kills the harmful substances. Bleach helps kill the bacteria and viruses in the wash; so does disinfecting the washing machine by running an empty load of just detergent and bleach. In about 50% of homes surveyed, fecal matter was found in family washing machines. No studies have been done on laundromats.

LENT IN WARM WEATHER: Aggressive, disease-carrying mosquitoes have

[W A S H I N G   M A C H I N E]

invaded the U.S. **DO NOT USE THE SAME BATH TOWEL TWICE:** Sloughed-

Caffeine has caused some deaths, usually preceded by delirium, seizures, and panic attacks. Drinking five to six cups of coffee per day made without a paper filter (such as cappuccino or espresso drinks) can raise levels of LDL (or bad) cholesterol. Caffeine also causes the tiny blood vessels in the eyes to constrict, making it harder for the eye to clean itself.

FRIGHT 🐦 BITE!

Doctors initially fail to diagnose 1 in 10 cases of appendicitis; up to a third of appendectomies remove a healthy appendix.

off skin cells contain bacteria and fungus, which thrive on a towel. DO NOT

Don't worry about shaking hands with that sneezy, sniffly guy you just met. Studies show that you are twice as likely to catch a cold virus from a phone book, a table, or some other inanimate object that an infected person has touched (door-knobs are especially suspect). Viruses can live in humid climates for up to five weeks, and a tenth of tabletop-dwelling viruses can be infectious.

FRIGHT 🐲 BITE!

Heavy rains and flooding can contaminate municipal and regional water supplies. The last century has been rainier than usual, contributing to the increase in water-borne diseases.

STORE MEDICINES IN A MEDICINE CABINET: The bathroom is a warm, moist

Women in their 20s and 30s and asthmatics are most vulnerable to sick building syndrome, which occurs when there is poor ventilation in offices.

FRIGHT 🦜 BITE!

Men are four times more likely to have an abdominal aneurysm (a dilated blood vessel) than women. They are most prevalent in Caucasians aged 50 to 80.

More than 23 million Americans, one million under 18, have lost some of their hearing. Researchers blame a third of those cases on noises in life: music, planes, lawnmowers, movies, or sandblasting. Loud noises destroy the tiny hairs on the inside of the ear. Once gone, those hairs never regrow. A ringing in the ears—tinnitus—affects 2 out of 10 people at some time. Causes are unclear, though loud noises, too much earwax, sinus infections, an underactive thyroid, and head and neck injuries may contribute.

FRIGHT 🦟 BITE!

Moving is a trigger for depression, unease, and a sense of impending doom. One out of five Americans moves every year.

A small unraised mole on your left calf starts looking strange:

You now just have a bigger, uglier mole.

It's the first stage of skin cancer, but the mole can easily be removed.

Flesh-eating bacteria have moved in; the limb may have to be removed.

SYMPTOM CHECK

Overexposure to certain compounds in common substances such as pigeon droppings, moldy hay, air conditioners, and coffee beans can result in hyper-sensitive lungs. The illness begins with coughing, chills, and fever and may lead to respiratory failure.

HANDS AFTER VISITING A DOCTOR: Medical offices specialize in germ traffic.

Lice

Ten to 12 million Americans, often children, get head lice annually. Lice are starting to become resistant to lice shampoo. Lice, which feed on blood, carry typhus and are responsible for spreading tularemia between humans. Tularemia causes headache, chills, and sweating, then lesions at the infection site. But lice have not always been so reviled. When Hernando Cortés came to Mexico, he noted that people cleaned lice off themselves, put them in little bags, and gave them to the king. And in northern Siberia, young women used to throw lice at men they found attractive.

GARGLE AND WASH YOUR HANDS AFTER KISSING A CHILD: Children,

Ticks

A tick is a bloodsucking arachnid that attaches itself to animals. Ticks secrete chemicals that numb the skin around the bite, so the host will not notice their presence. About 200 species of ticks inhabit the United States. Depending upon the kind of tick, the female will lay between 100 and 6,000 eggs per batch. Ticks carry Lyme disease, Rocky Mountain spotted fever, tularemia, and relapsing fever. A new tick-borne disease was recently discovered. Carried by the lone-star ticks, it is more common in the southern United States, and resembles and is treated similarly to Lyme disease. Some ticks also cause anorexia and lethargy, and, in some cases, paralysis. One deer tick can carry the bacteria or parasite for two out of three diseases: Lyme disease, H.G.E (or human granulocytic ehrlichiosis) and babesiosis. Researchers expect to soon find a tick carrying all three bacteria.

because they are closer to the ground and put their hands in their mouths,

FRIGHT 🦜 BITE!

Rainy hot summers increase the lifespan and potency of fungus and bacteria.

Diarrhea can be caused by eating too much diet food. Also, apple and pear juice and some sugar-free gum and candy that contain sorbitol, hexitols, and mannitol can be responsible.

FRIGHT 🦜 BITE!

Seven percent of U.S. watersheds are contaminated. Eating fish caught in these areas can be unhealthy. Most contaminated areas are near urban and industrial areas.

are germ carriers. ALWAYS PUT IN EARPLUGS WHEN AN AMBULANCE, FIRE

The condition neurasthenia, or feeling **easily fatigued, lacking motivation, and feeling inadequate**, was rampant among the American intellectual and economic elite around the first World War. Those afflicted include Teddy Roosevelt, Emma Goldman, Henry James, and Edith Wharton, who ended up writing in bed.

FRIGHT 🦎 BITE!

Smoking both cigarettes and pot give you a much higher chance of getting lung cancer than cigarettes alone.

Toxoplasmosis is transmitted through cat feces and undercooked meat. The cat box is a toxoplasmosis danger spot; pregnant women and their fetuses are vulnerable. If not diagnosed—and often there are no symptoms—pregnant women with toxoplasmosis can pass the disease to their unborn babies, which can result in blindness and mental retardation.

TRUCK, OR POLICE CAR APPROACHES OR WHEN YOU ARE NEAR AN AIR-

FRIGHT 🐦 BITE!

More than 10% of school children are classified as clinically maladjusted.

In 1985, 16,000 Chicago residents got food poisoning by drinking milk that contained *Salmonella*. Two weeks later, 2% of those people developed chronic arthritis.

FRIGHT 🐦 BITE!

One half of all antibiotics sold in the United States go into animal feed.

Contact dermatitis is responsible for more than half of all work-related illness (not including injury). One out of a thousand employed Americans suffers from this skin disorder.

PORT: Loud noises contribute to hearing loss. DO NOT BE RUDE TO YOUR

The fungus *Candida albicans* lives in every human being, and is responsible for yeast infections in women. But in very sick people with damaged immune systems, candida can be deadly, leading to blindness, heart failure, and disastrous blood clotting. Candida infections can then spread to other, less ill people in hospitals through catheters and infected equipment. Incidence of the fungus has doubled in the last decade.

FRIGHT BITE!

It is possible to get crabs from a toilet seat, as well as from a sauna.

WAITER: Revenge tactics such as spitting into food or drinks are common.

Mercury vapor lamps are used most often in gymnasiums, banks, and stores. If broken but still used, they can cause corneal burns, headaches, nausea, diarrhea, and double vision.

FRIGHT 🐓 BITE!

On average, paperwork accounts for more than a quarter of a hospital's budget.

FRIGHT 🦜 BITE!

The state of Massachusetts passed a law in 1997 that guaranteed health coverage to anyone who could pay—despite existing health conditions. Immediately following that change, 20 insurance carriers ceased insuring in the state. Many of the remaining companies increased their rates, some quadrupling their prices.

One percent of the population is sensitive to sulfites, substances sprayed on food to prevent it from spoiling. Five percent of those with asthma may have severe reactions to sulfites. Scientists do not know how concentrated the sulfites must be to cause a reaction. Sulfites may be present in wine, on fruit, in some drugs, on shrimp and lobster, and can cause hives, difficulty breathing, and, in rare cases, irregular heart beats.

FRIGHT 🦜 BITE!

Gums that have grown down over the teeth may signal leukemia.

Whooping cough is on the rise, and 90% of all cases go undiagnosed. DO

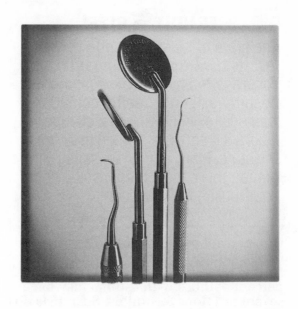

[D E N T A L   T O O L S]

NOT SWALLOW WATER IN A RIVER, LAKE, JACUZZI, OR SWIMMING POOL: The

If you have any **PHOBIAS** at all, chances are you have odontiato-phobia—fear of dentists.

FRIGHT 🐦 BITE!

5% of makeup counter samples in department stores were found to be contaminated with fungus and other organisms.

Although there are hundreds of antibiotics, only about a dozen antifungal medicines exist. Because the structure of fungal cells is similar to that of human cells, fungal medications can have a tendency to be rather toxic, often with painful side effects. Maybe athlete's foot isn't so bad after all.

FRIGHT 🐦 BITE!

Bacteria flourish in sponges. People who are neater tend to wipe off surfaces more often, spreading bacteria throughout their kitchen.

ronments. DO NOT KEEP YOUR TOOTHBRUSH IN AN EXPOSED HOLDER OR

Your face flushes and you have a burning feeling in your chest:

You could be in love and about to tell your date how you feel.

You could be having an allergic reaction to MSG. It will pass in a few minutes, though it may make you tired.

You could be having a heart attack.

Q FEVER, characterized by high fever, chills, and muscular pain, is transmitted through ticks, flies, birds— and the air.

CUP: Sinks and particularly toilets spew germ-infested droplets into the air.

Useful Numbers

American Psychological Association
(202) 336-5500
www.apa.org/

American Psychiatric Association
(202) 682-6000
www.psych.org/

Freedom From Fear, Inc.
(718) 351-1717

National Mental Health Association
(800) 969-6642
www.nmha.org/

Phobics Anonymous
(760) 322-2673

National Alliance for the Mentally Ill
(800) 950-6264

Anxiety Disorders Unit— National Institutes of Mental Health
(888) 826-9438
www.nimh.nih.gov/anxiety/index.htm

Anxiety Disorders Association of America
(301) 231-9350
www.adaa.org

National Institute for Occupational Safety and Health
(800) 356-4674

The Food Allergy Network
(703) 691-3179

American Academy of Allergy and Immunology
(414) 272-6071

Allergy Referral Hotline
(800) 822-ASMA

Then the sixth prize was awarded and it went to the holder of the ticket numbered 8662-71-4923.

It was a rosebush, a slightly dried out rosebush wrapped in burlap with a card attached carrying instructions for planting and showing a picture of a full-blown scarlet rose, one of the dozens promised when the bush would finally bloom.

A rosebush. Of all good things on earth, a rosebush. The whole world set up a singing as Georgie clutched the prize against his chest. "The best prize in the world," he whispered to Mrs. Sims who closed her eyes as her mind raced through all the difficulties Georgie was bound to encounter in caring for this best prize in the world.